UNFORGETTABLE LESSONS

EZ Lesson Plan

THE VISUAL BIBLE

A Study of the Sermon on the Mount in the Gospel of Matthew

Participant's Guide

Neil Wilson

Nelson
multi media group
A THOMAS NELSON COMPANY

A Thomas Nelson Company
www.thomasnelson.com

Unforgettable Lessons *Participant's Guide*
EZ Lesson Plan
The Visual Bible

Copyright © 2002 Nelson Multi Media Group.

Published by Nelson Multi Media Group, a Division of Thomas Nelson, Inc., P.O. Box 141000, Nashville, Tennessee, 37214.

Scripture passages taken from:

The Holy Bible, New International Version (NIV). Copyright © 1973, 1978, 1984 by International Bible Society. Used by permission of Zondervan Bible Publishers.

The Holy Bible, New King James Version (NKJV). Copyright © 1979, 1980, 1982 by Thomas Nelson, Inc. Used by permission. All rights reserved.

The Holy Bible, New Century Version (NCV). Copyright © 1987, 1988, 1991 by Word Publishing, Dallas, Texas 75234. Used by permission.

Scripture text taken from the NEW INTERNATIONAL VERSION® of the Bible. Copyright 1974, 1979, 1984 by International Bible Society. All rights reserved. The NEW INTERNATIONAL VERSION® text edited for screenplay by permission of International Bible Society.

All photos are taken from *Matthew* featuring actor Bruce Marchiano (Jesus) and the photography of Robby Botha. These photos are used by permission and are copyright by Visual Bible International, Inc.

Produced with the assistance of The Livingstone Corporation. Project staff includes Neil Wilson, Paige Drygas, Ashley Taylor, Katie Gieser, and Andrea Reider. Design by Mark Wainwright.

ISBN 0-8499-8941-8

Printed in the United States of America

CONTENTS

WELCOME AND INTRODUCTION FOR PARTICIPANTS

- When you open your Bible, does God speak to you?
- Can you remember the last time you heard the Scriptures read well in a public setting?
- How often have you been in a Bible study where the emphasis was on what the Bible actually said rather than on what people in the group thought?

Welcome to this EZ Lesson study of *The Visual Bible.*

When the Apostle Paul wrote to his partner Timothy about the priorities of ministry, he gave his young apprentice the following instructions: "Until I come, **devote yourself to the public reading of Scripture,** to preaching and to teaching" (1 Tim. 4:13 NIV, emphasis added). If that short list of actions–public reading, preaching, and teaching–was meant to suggest time allotments, it would mean that a third of the time should be spent in the public reading of Scripture. That's probably not what Paul had in mind, but the fact is that in a world with few books and no printing press, the public reading of Scripture was a highlight of Christian gatherings.

Because their attention spans were not overwhelmed from every direction, believers in earlier times were better listeners. They didn't have computers, records, and CD burners to back up their memories, so their memories were alert, their senses were sharp, and they simply paid better attention to what they saw and heard. Compared to them, we need help. Our attention spans continue to shrink. *The Visual Bible* meets us not only where our media training has brought us, but it also takes us back into the Bible text. It can increase our concentration!

The Visual Bible reintroduces us to the panorama of God's Word. It opens to us the scenes of Scripture. It reemphasizes in a fresh way the importance of the context of specific statements in the Bible. "Reading" *The Visual Bible* gives us a broadened and deepened experience of Scripture.

At first, you may feel like you are missing a lot as you watch and listen. Don't get discouraged. Work on paying attention and using your open Bible to back up your attention span. You will gradually find yourself using the Bible less to see what you missed and more to confirm your recollection. Repeated use of *The Visual Bible* will greatly aid your efforts to memorize Scripture.

EZ Lesson *Visual Bible* Study Components

You will find the following components in each lesson, listed with their primary purpose:

- **Introduction**–Background information on the theme of the lesson.
- **Sidebars**–Remarkable quotes and helpful definitions related to the lesson and highlighted within the lesson.
- **To Get Started**–Warm-up questions for group interaction.
- **Host**–The role of the host is primarily twofold:
  1. to offer, not commentary, but context comments to prepare the viewer for the text; and
  2. to create a bridge over the gap between visual texts that we don't notice as much when we turn pages in our printed Bibles.
- **Watching the Word**–View *The Visual Bible* Scripture passages for the session.
- **Scripture**–While the theme of the study may focus on a verse or statement within a larger text of the Bible, *The Visual Bible* portions have been selected to present a complete thought or scene within Scripture.

- **First Impressions**—Review and record your immediate response to the Scripture passages.
- **Second Look**—Note, with the help of your Bible, the details of the passages.
- **Observations**—Reflect more deeply on the significance and the lessons of these passages.
- **Conclusions**—Bring the lessons from Scripture into your life by thoughtful application.
- **Choices**—Make decisions about your response to the lesson, and implement the applications you have discovered.
- **Roadside Conversations**—Brief, optional daily review studies related to the Bible passages in the lesson.

May you find your experience of *The Visual Bible* an igniting or reigniting process that makes the study of God's Word a passion in your life.

EZ LESSONS
VISUAL BIBLE HOST
DR. DAVID JEREMIAH

The Role of the Host

In the EZ Lesson *Visual Bible* studies, the host helps to introduce the various passages of Scripture in each session. His role is not to "teach" the passages but to give some sense of the context, provide a bridge between video clips, and prepare the group for the discussion to follow. Again, the primary purpose of these studies is to expose people to God's Word in a way that will spur them on to further study.

About the Host

Nelson Multi Media Group is pleased to welcome Dr. David Jeremiah as host of *The Visual Bible* EZ Lessons, Unforgettable Lessons. For those unfamiliar with Dr. Jeremiah's extensive writing, radio, television, and speaking ministry, the following will help introduce our host for this *Visual Bible* study.

Dr. David Jeremiah is Senior Pastor of Shadow Mountain Community Church in El Cajon, California. For ten years he served as President of Christian Heritage College in El Cajon. In 1998, he was appointed Chancellor. Dr. Jeremiah is also the host of the national radio program *Turning Point*.

Having a wealth of pastoral experience, Dr. Jeremiah has served as a member of the pastoral staff at Haddon Heights Baptist Church in Haddon Heights, New Jersey. He was the founder of Blackhawk Baptist Church in Fort Wayne, Indiana, which grew from twelve families to thirteen hundred members in twelve years.

Along with his experience in the pastorate, Dr. Jeremiah has launched television and radio programs, including *The Bible Hour,* seen in five major markets in the Indiana area. *Turning Point*, a national daily radio program, is broadcast on more than one thousand stations. He was also the recipient of the Broadcaster of the Year Award for 2000 from the National Religious Broadcasters. Since 1996, Dr. Jeremiah has served on the board of directors for the National Religious Broadcasters.

Dr. Jeremiah is also a regular guest speaker at Moody Bible Institute's Pastors' Conference, Alumni Week, and Founder's Week. Dr. Jeremiah holds a B.A. from Cedarville College, Cedarville, Ohio; a Th.M. from Dallas Theological Seminary; and a Doctorate of Divinity, also from Cedarville.

He has coauthored, with Carole Carlson, two best-selling Word books, *Escape the Coming Night* and *The Handwriting on the Wall,* which focus on the meaning of biblical prophecy. *Escape the Coming Night* was rereleased in 1998. *Jesus' Final Warning* (Word, June 1999), nominated for the Gold Medallion Award, examines what Jesus told His followers about the end times. Other books include *Turning Toward Joy, Turning Toward Integrity, The Power of Encouragement,* and *Gifts from God.*

Following the best-selling *A Bend in the Road* (Word, September 2000), Jeremiah has recently released his latest book, *Turning Points* (W Group, 2001).

Dr. Jeremiah and his wife, Donna, have four children: Janice, David Michael, Jennifer, and Daniel.

ABOUT *THE VISUAL BIBLE*

The Visual Bible, Gospel of Matthew, is a genuine version of part of God's Word. With the exception of the introduction to Matthew, every word of the "script" used by the actors comes directly from the New International Version of the Bible, one of the most widely used texts of Scripture in English. You will note that the chapter and verse numbers are provided in the lower right-hand corner of the screen, so you can easily follow along in your printed Bible text.

The objective of *The Visual Bible* is to eventually offer a highly creative, accurate, filmed version of the entire Bible. Several books have already been completed. They are having a definite impact on the way people experience God's Word.

You will probably find at least three big and refreshing differences between reading your Bible as a book and "reading" *The Visual Bible.*

The first is that when we read the printed page, our eyes lose track of the time that is passing in the story. We can read in less than a second a series of actions that may have taken hours or days. *The Visual Bible* forces us to change the pace of reading. When Jesus got into a boat, He didn't do it instantly. Jesus multiplied bread and fish in a flash, but feeding five thousand people actually took a little longer. You're about to feel and see that difference. *The Visual Bible* brings the Scripture to us in a way that reminds us that God's Word is not just words on a page, but God's story lived out in the experiences of women and men just like us.

The second difference about *The Visual Bible* is that it informs and corrects some of our mental pictures of events in Scripture. It fills our minds with background scenes from the Middle East and reminds us that Jesus lived in a crowded environment. There were people everywhere!

The third refreshing difference in Matthew's Gospel of *The Visual Bible* is the way that Bruce Marchiano, the actor who played Jesus, chose to present the Savior. You are about to spend time with an obviously joyful Jesus. Some people have a mental picture of Jesus that simply denies the possibility that He ever smiled. They seem to think that He would have failed, somehow, if He had ever laughed! They like to quote the shortest verse in the Bible—"Jesus wept (John 11:35, NIV)—as if that's all He did. The fact that John made it a point to say that Jesus wept may also indicate that tears were actually an unusual response. Jesus didn't cry a lot. It is difficult to imagine that a somber and unsmiling Jesus would have attracted crowds and children the way He did! After using *The Visual Bible,* you may find yourself reading your printed Bible with the intention of thinking of Jesus smiling as often as possible.

One further note about the style of presentation that will help you sort out what you are seeing: *The Visual Bible, Gospel of Matthew* is presented in two parallel time frames. The old disciple Matthew, played by Richard Kiley, is dictating his Gospel to scribes or, on occasion, he is writing sections himself. At other times, we are actually watching what he is dictating. Be aware that the time frames can change abruptly. Sometimes Kiley's voice narrates what we see Jesus doing. Once this is understood, it actually helps us appreciate the way in which the Scriptures may have first been recorded.

If this is your introduction to *The Visual Bible,* enjoy this experiential version of God's Word. Allow yourself to witness what the original participants saw, heard, and felt as God prepared His message for the world.

THE BIG PICTURE

Key Question for This Lesson:
In what ways do the Beatitudes summarize the Christian life?

introduction

"The Lord is my . . . "
   "Our Father . . . "
   "Blessed are . . . "
   Certain phrases seem to stay with us from the first time we hear them. Many of us can identify the Shepherd's Psalm, the Lord's Prayer, and the Beatitudes even if we don't know where they are found in the Bible. We learn their words as little children and sometimes, especially when we face hardship, sorrow, and loss, the words and phrases come back to us with comfort, stability, and hope. People who don't know the Shepherd seem to want to hear Psalm 23; people who don't pray will often find themselves saying the Lord's Prayer with others; and people who have never met Jesus seem drawn by those repeated phrases, "Blessed are . . . Blessed are . . . Blessed are. . . ." This longing for deeply moving words that carry a certain message may indicate an almost unquenchable thirst in the human soul for God's blessing. Those who know the Lord discover they also have a Shepherd; those who know the King find He is also their Heavenly Father; and those who follow and believe in Jesus receive a life of blessing.

Notice, as you hear and study the Beatitudes, that they form a "round." The first and the last promises are identical. Both the poor in spirit and the persecuted share ownership of the kingdom of heaven. This is one of the indications that the list may not be a random group of spiritual goals but a specific progression of spiritual growth. Consider that possibility as you reflect on Jesus' words. The key question you will be considering throughout this lesson is, "In what ways do the Beatitudes summarize the Christian life?" Perhaps a good follow-up question would be, "Which beatitude best describes the present condition of your relationship with God?"

THE POWER
AND THE
PRESENCE
Visual Bible Study

> Some people feel that the Sermon really wasn't a sermon, but a number of Jesus' sayings which the early church collected and put together. This may be true; we just don't know. The main thing, however, is that Jesus said them, whether in one discourse or many. They are genuine, and being His, are authoritative. It is my belief that instead of being a collection of sayings, the Sermon is a *condensation* of a much longer discourse. We do know that multitudes continued with Him for as long as three days at a time (Matt. 15:32), and while He did much healing then, He no doubt also used the opportunity to teach and pray at great length.
>
> ~Clarence Jordan[1]

To Get Started

Before a sermon begins, the audience is often restless, wondering what they will hear. The multitude that gathered on the hillside with Jesus one day probably had the same thoughts. They were curious about Jesus. They marveled at His actions. They were impressed by His growing reputation. And they waited expectantly, hoping He might have something memorable to tell them. The following questions will help you clarify your expectations and think a little about the experiences, good and bad, that you have had while listening to sermons.

• What would be your candidates for the two or three most unforgettable sermons you ever heard?

_____

_____

_____

_____

_____

_____

_____

_____

• Describe several characteristics that you think make a sermon or a preacher most effective and memorable.

_____

_____

_____

_____

_____

_____

_____

_____

• What differences are there between memorable sermons and effective sermons, and if you could choose to hear one or the other, which would you prefer?

_____

_____

_____

_____

_____

_____

_____

_____

Watching the Word
The Visual Bible "Reading" 1

As host David Jeremiah notes in his opening words, "In chapters 5, 6, and 7 of Matthew we find the longest continual quotation from Jesus that Matthew recorded in his Gospel. We call it the Sermon on the Mount." For these *Visual Bible* studies, we are focusing on the unforgettable lessons Jesus taught in these three highly concentrated chapters. As our host points out, "You are about to experience the Sermon on the Mount, not only as the words of Scripture, but with some powerful suggestions about what the first audience heard, saw, and felt when Jesus first spoke these words."

○ Video Segment: Matthew 4:25—5:48
  Study Text: The setting and the first third of the Sermon on the Mount

The Beatitudes: Another Contemporary Bible Version

Those people who know they have great spiritual needs are happy,
    because the kingdom of heaven belongs to them.
Those who are sad now are happy,
    because God will comfort them.
Those who are humble are happy,
    because the earth will belong to them.
Those who want to do right more than anything else are happy,
    because God will fully satisfy them.
Those who show mercy to others are happy,
    because God will show mercy to them.
Those who are pure in their thinking are happy,
    because they will be with God.
Those who work to bring peace are happy,
    because God will call them his children.
Those who are treated badly for doing good are happy,
    because the kingdom of heaven belongs to them.
○ Matthew 5:3–10 (NCV)

First Impressions

Try to answer the next two questions without referring to your Bible or a printed text.

• What did you notice about the way Jesus delivered the Beatitudes in *The Visual Bible* format compared to simply hearing the text read aloud?

_____

_____

_____

_____

_____

_____

_____

_____

_____

_____

_____

_____

_____

• How many of the Beatitudes can you list from memory?

The eight specific terms of the Beatitudes in the NIV are . . .

1.

_____

_____

_____

2.

_____

_____

_____

3.

_____

_____

_____

4.

_____

_____

_____

5.

_____

_____

_____

6.

_____

_____

_____

7.

_____

_____

_____

8.

_____

_____

_____

• Now, can you list the particular blessing next to each character trait above?

_____

_____

_____

• What is your definition or understanding of the words "beatitude" and "blessing"?

_____

_____

_____

_____

> *Beatitude* is actually the transliterated Latin term (that means we borrowed it and added an English sound) which means blessing.
>
> *Blessing* translates a Greek word that combines the idea of large size with the idea of fortune or happiness. "The Greek word was used in Greek literature, in the Septuagint (the Greek translation of the Old Testament), and in the New Testament to describe the kind of happiness that comes from receiving divine favor. The word can be rendered *happy*. In the New Testament it is usually passive; God is the One who is blessing or favoring the person."
>
> ~*Source:* The Nelson Study Bible,[2] *copyright © 1997 by Thomas Nelson, Inc. Used by permission.*

Second Look

Now, using your Bible, work on the following questions. The focus of this lesson will be limited to Matthew 5:1–12.

• Write a brief description of each of the character traits that underlie the Beatitudes.

Poor in spirit

_____

_____

_____

_____

_____

_____

_____

_____

_____

_____

_____

Mourn

_____

_____

_____

_____

_____

_____

_____

_____

_____

_____

_____

Meek

_____

_____

_____

_____

_____

_____

_____

_____

_____

_____

_____

Hunger and thirst

_____

_____

_____

_____

_____

_____

_____

_____

_____

_____

_____

_____

_____

Merciful

_____
_____
_____
_____
_____
_____
_____
_____
_____
_____

Purity

_____
_____
_____
_____
_____
_____
_____
_____
_____
_____
_____
_____

Peacemaking

_____
_____
_____
_____
_____
_____
_____
_____
_____
_____
_____
_____

Persecuted

_____
_____
_____
_____
_____
_____
_____
_____
_____
_____

- Refer below to the list called The Unbeatitudes. How does looking at the opposites of the Beatitudes help you understand the significance of what Jesus was describing?

_____
_____
_____
_____
_____
_____
_____
_____
_____
_____
_____

> **The Unbeatitudes**
>
> We can understand the Beatitudes by looking at them from their opposites. Some, Jesus implied, will not be blessed. Their condition could be described in this way:
>
> Wretched are the spiritually self-sufficient, for theirs is the kingdom of hell.
>
> Wretched are those who deny the tragedy of their sinfulness, for they will be troubled.
>
> Wretched are the self-centered, for they will be empty.
>
> Wretched are those who ceaselessly justify themselves, for their efforts will be in vain.
>
> Wretched are the merciless, for no mercy will be shown to them.
>
> Wretched are those with impure hearts, for they will not see God.
>
> Wretched are those who reject peace, for they will earn the title "sons of Satan."
>
> Wretched are the uncommitted for convenience's sake, for their destination is hell.
>
> ~*Source:* Life Application Bible Commentary: Matthew[3]

Observations

The following questions are intended to help you move from general questions about the passage to specific questions that will help you prepare to apply the teachings of Jesus to your life.

- As you examine the list of Beatitudes, which ones seem to emphasize the internal, private aspects of our relationship with God? Which ones emphasize the external, public aspects of our relationship with God? Place an X under the appropriate answer for each of the Beatitudes.

	Internal Responses	External Experiences
Poor in spirit		
Mourn		
Meek		
Hunger and thirst		
Merciful		
Pure in heart		
Peacemakers		
Persecuted		

- Some look at the Beatitudes and describe them as spiritual milestones, levels of spiritual development that we pass through in developing maturity. Others describe the Beatitudes as ongoing character traits always under development that may receive intense attention at certain times in our lives. How would you describe the Beatitudes?

_____

_____

_____

_____

_____

_____

_____

_____

_____

_____

_____

_____

_____

- If you had been sitting with the crowd on the mountainside that day, which of the Beatitudes would you have asked Jesus to talk about more? Why?

_____

_____

_____

_____

_____

_____

_____

_____

_____

Conclusions

The following questions invite you to apply the truth of the Beatitudes to your life. They will provide you with a starting place as you seek to take seriously the big picture that Jesus presented that day.

- How many of the Beatitudes can you identify in your own life at the present time? Beside each quality listed below, rate yourself on a scale of 1 to 5, with 1 being low and 5 high.

  Poor in spirit

  Mourn

  Meek

  Hunger and thirst

  Merciful

  Pure in heart

  Peacemakers

  Persecuted

- Up until now, which two Beatitudes have presented the greatest spiritual challenge in your life?

_____

_____

_____

_____

_____

_____

_____

_____

_____

_____

_____

_____

_____

_____

_____

_____

_____

Choices

These final questions will usually be answered in private. If time remains in your group discussion, you may want to share part of your answers with the others as a way to ask for their prayer support.

• Which of the Beatitudes would you most like to see more clearly in your relationship with God?

_____

_____

_____

_____

_____

_____

_____

_____

_____

_____

_____

_____

_____

_____

_____

_____

_____

_____

_____

_____

• What two actions will you take in the next several days to consciously put into practice the attitudes in the Beatitudes?

_____

_____

_____

_____

_____

_____

_____

_____

_____

_____

_____

_____

_____

_____

_____

_____

_____

_____

_____

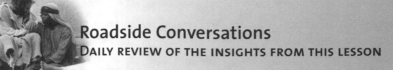

Roadside Conversations
DAILY REVIEW OF THE INSIGHTS FROM THIS LESSON

Daily Roadside Conversation 1
"Deep Change"

READ: Matthew 5:1–12

Reflect on this key question:

How serious have I been about actually following Jesus and imitating Him in the way that I live?

_____

_____

_____

_____

_____

_____

_____

_____

_____

_____

_____

_____

_____

_____

_____

Resolve to return often to the Beatitudes with the intention of asking God to make you the kind of person those qualities describe.

Suggested prayer: Lord Jesus, pour and build into me a continual willingness to acknowledge my spiritual poverty and mourn in clear repentance; to grow in humility and deeply desire righteousness; to practice mercy and maintain transparency; to pursue peace and endure in a fallen world. I will need Your help every moment, and I ask for it in Your name, Jesus. Amen.

Daily Roadside Conversation 2
"Two Steps into Humility: Poverty of Spirit and Mourning"

READ: Matthew 5:1–12

Reflect on this key question:

Have I ever clearly and consciously responded to God's invitation to be in intimate relationship with Him by admitting my spiritual bankruptcy, repenting, and accepting God's forgiveness and grace?

_____

_____

_____

_____

_____

_____

_____

_____

_____

_____

_____

_____

Resolve to describe to at least one other person this week how you first came to acknowledge Jesus Christ as Savior and Lord.

Suggested prayer: Savior, I admit my own sinfulness. I grieve for my sins—for those I willfully committed and those I unconsciously committed. I ask You for wisdom to initiate reconciliation and restitution in those relationships where my spiritual poverty has harmed others. I freely recognize, perhaps as never before, that I need a Savior—Someone who can pay the debt I can never pay. I know, Jesus, that You are that One. Thank you.

Daily Roadside Conversation 3
"Two Deep Desires: Meekness and Hunger and Thirst for Righteousness"
READ: Matthew 5:1–12
Reflect on this key question:
How do meekness (turning away from certain desires) and the hunger and thirst for righteousness (turning toward other desires) balance each other in the life of someone who is following Jesus?

_____
_____
_____
_____
_____
_____
_____
_____
_____
_____
_____

Resolve to identify and reject self-centered tendencies, and strongly desire to see God-centered decisions take place in your life and sphere of influence.

Suggested prayer: Lord Jesus, You are my Shepherd, so I have everything I need. You promise to satisfy all my hungers and to lead me in ways that demonstrate righteousness because that is Your character. Remind me daily to turn away from what is my will and seek to see Your will be done. In Your name, Jesus. Amen.

Daily Roadside Conversation 4
"Outlooks: Mercy and Purity of Heart"
READ: Matthew 5:1–12
Reflect on this key question:
To what degree do the people closest to me know me as a person who is quick to exercise mercy and purity of heart?

_____
_____
_____
_____
_____
_____
_____
_____
_____
_____
_____
_____

Resolve to identify relationships in which your lack of mercy or purity of heart has caused harm. Ask God to provide opportunities for reconciliation.

Suggested prayer: Jesus, Your first thought from the cross was to forgive those who put You there, including me. Others who have followed You have demonstrated that same quality of mercy. I know my heart is a dark place without You, full of impurity and vengefulness. I renew my desire to have You clean me up inside, giving me a capacity for mercy and purity that I know comes only from You. Thank you, Lord.

Daily Roadside Conversation 5
"An Unfair Exchange: Peacemaking for Persecution"
READ: Matthew 5:1–12
Reflect on this key question:
How clearly do I understand and accept the fact that if I am faithful to Jesus as I live my life, I will not be accepted by the world?

_____

_____

_____

_____

_____

_____

_____

_____

_____

_____

_____

Resolve to look for opportunities today to be a voice for peace in your home, school, and workplace.

Suggested prayer: Lord, help me not to think of my little problems as persecution. I pray for brothers and sisters in other places of the world who truly are suffering and dying because they represent You. Strengthen and bless them. Help me to be as faithful in my comfortable surroundings. And if difficulties come, remind me to rejoice and be glad! In Your name, Jesus. Amen.

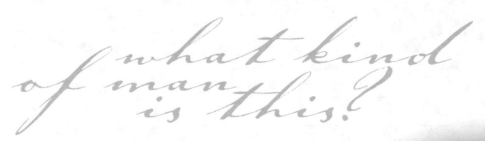

what kind of man is this?

LIFE IN THE SPOTLIGHT

Key Question for This Lesson:
What were Jesus' central relationship guidelines for His followers?

introduction

"I'm talking to you!"

In the Sermon on the Mount, Jesus frequently addressed His listeners, and us, with devastating directness. Particularly as we hear His words spoken with such deliberation from the screen, they reach out to us. They demand a moral response. We can try to excuse or exempt ourselves from His teaching, but the effort we make indicates that the words have found their mark in our lives. We know Jesus was talking *about* us. We know He was talking *to* us.

The six paragraphs that follow the Beatitudes focus on aspects of our most intimate relationships. Jesus begins with comments about the expected effect that His followers are to have on the world. He calls us to be light. But as the practical and difficult aspects of following Jesus become clear, it also becomes apparent that we are living in the spotlight. Not only does the world examine who we are in comparison with who we claim to be, but God also watches to see whether or not our lives match our claims.

This continuous awareness of God's observation of and participation in our lives elicits two distinct responses from us: 1) a heightened awareness of our shortcomings, and 2) a deepened appreciation for God's grace. We are under God's spotlight for our own good. The specific guidelines offered by Christ come in the context of His ongoing involvement with us. Every relationship in our lives also involves our relationship with Jesus.

THE POWER
AND THE
PRESENCE
Visual Bible Study

Salt in the Roman world symbolized purity—no doubt from the process of using sea water and the sun to acquire the salt. Roman soldiers were often paid in salt, the basis for the word "salary." Jesus' use of the symbol of salt to describe the disciples emphasizes the call and influence of purity the Christian brings to society. But salt was also a preservative in a day without refrigeration. This meaning is expressed in Jesus' warning about salt that has lost its savor (Luke 14:34–35). Meat spoiled unless it was salted. Similarly, the Kingdom member is a preserving element in society.

~Myron Augsburger[1]

To Get Started

Use one or more of the questions below to begin to focus your thinking on the themes of this session. Use the lines provided to jot down ideas, and be prepared to share with others in the group.

- Write out a brief definition of the word *commitment*.

_____
_____
_____
_____
_____
_____

- In what ways does commitment affect relationships?

_____
_____
_____
_____
_____

- Most of us collect memorable phrases as we go through life. Significant people say certain things over and over until we can hardly think of them without hearing those phrases. Some are funny; many are wise. What are some examples of memorable phrases from your personal collection?

_____
_____
_____
_____
_____

- Other than the Beatitudes from the last lesson, what short sound bites or phrases come to mind when you think of Jesus' memorable quotes?

_____
_____
_____
_____

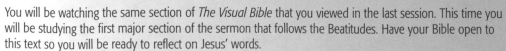

Watching the Word
The Visual Bible "Reading" 2

You will be watching the same section of *The Visual Bible* that you viewed in the last session. This time you will be studying the first major section of the sermon that follows the Beatitudes. Have your Bible open to this text so you will be ready to reflect on Jesus' words.

The theme for this lesson is "Six Insights from Jesus about Personal Relationships." As you experience the words of Jesus, try to identify the six insights about personal relationships that He gave the multitude that day. You will have an opportunity to talk about them later in the session.

○ Video Segment: Matthew 4:25—6:34
○ Study Text: Matthew 5:13–37

> **Another Perspective on Matthew 5:33–37**
> "And don't say anything you don't mean. This counsel is embedded deep in our traditions. You only make things worse when you lay down a smoke screen of pious talk, saying, 'I'll pray for you,' and never doing it, or saying, 'God be with you,' and not meaning it. You don't make your words true by embellishing them with religious lace. In making your speech sound more religious, it becomes less true. Just say 'yes' and 'no.' When you manipulate words to get your own way, you go wrong."
> ~*Eugene Peterson*[2]

First Impressions

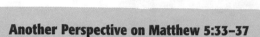

This section explores the difference between our typical approach to Bible study (reading a written text) and studying *The Visual Bible*. Keep notes of your reactions and responses to Jesus' audiovisual presentation of this part of the Sermon on the Mount.

• What did you notice/remember about the presentation of each of the following sections in *The Visual Bible*? How were they different from just reading the text or your previous mental images of Jesus presenting these ideas?

5:13–16 Salt and Light

_____

_____

_____

_____

_____

_____

_____

5:17–20 Jesus on the Law

_____

_____

_____

_____

_____

_____

_____

_____

_____

5:21–26 Deadly Intent

_____
_____
_____
_____
_____
_____
_____

5:27–30 Adultery

_____
_____
_____
_____
_____
_____
_____
_____
_____
_____

5:31–32 Divorce

_____
_____
_____
_____
_____
_____
_____
_____
_____
_____

5:33–37 Promises

_____
_____
_____
_____
_____
_____
_____
_____

Second Look

One of the best ways to pay attention and stop casual reading when approaching the Bible is to summarize or paraphrase the central ideas in any passage. If you understand what is being said, you should be able to express it in your own words.

- Write out a brief summary of the main points in each of the sections:

5:13–16 Salt and Light
Jesus expected His disciples and followers to make an impact on the world. They were to provide the influence, not the other way around.

_____

_____

_____

_____

_____

_____

_____

_____

_____

5:17–20 Jesus on the Law
God has not changed His mind about human behavior. The original Law remains in place, though it has been "fulfilled" by Jesus. In other words, we don't measure our lives or try to earn God's acceptance by keeping the Law; instead we trust Christ and His help to live a righteous life.

_____

_____

_____

_____

_____

_____

_____

_____

_____

5:21–26 Deadly Intent
Internal attitudes and verbal expressions do have consequences and harmful effects. Whatever the cause of offense, Jesus urged His disciples to settle disputes and disagreements quickly.

_____

_____

_____

_____

_____

_____

_____

_____

_____

_____

5:27–30 Adultery

Lust is not a victimless crime. It reinforces a sinful attitude toward others and internally displays a willingness to disobey God's orders. It conditions a person for eventual outward sin.

_____

_____

_____

_____

_____

_____

_____

_____

_____

5:31–32 Divorce

Divorce is not condoned in Scripture as a handy way to reshuffle marital partners. God hates it (Mal. 2:16). While there may be cases in which divorce occurs (unfaithfulness), God's standard and expectation from His people is faithfulness in marriage.

_____

_____

_____

_____

_____

_____

_____

_____

_____

_____

_____

5:33–37 Promises

Keep your promises few, and make sure you keep your word once you have given it. Better to avoid a vow than to make one you don't intend to keep.

_____

_____

_____

_____

_____

_____

_____

_____

_____

_____

Observations

The focus of this lesson is to highlight the way Jesus' teaching affected relationships. People didn't follow Jesus in a vacuum; they brought with them all the challenges and struggles that come with living out relationships in a fallen world. That is why so many of His teachings had a direct relational component and application. Work through the list of topics again, making observations about the way in which Jesus' words related to personal relationships.

• What does each of these six sections have to say about relationships?

5:13–16 Salt and Light

_____

_____

_____

_____

_____

_____

_____

_____

_____

_____

5:17–20 Jesus on the Law

_____

_____

_____

_____

_____

_____

_____

_____

_____

_____

_____

5:21–26 Deadly Intent

_____

_____

_____

_____

_____

_____

_____

_____

_____

_____

_____

5:27–30 Adultery

_____
_____
_____
_____
_____
_____
_____
_____
_____
_____
_____

5:31–32 Divorce

_____
_____
_____
_____
_____
_____
_____
_____
_____
_____
_____
_____
_____
_____

5:33–37 Promises

_____
_____
_____
_____
_____
_____
_____
_____
_____
_____
_____
_____
_____

Conclusions

Eventually, Bible study takes root in our lives. The objective in reading and reflecting on God's Word is ultimately to lead us to act on what we have learned. Conclusions can follow the earlier parts of the lesson with the word, *therefore*. If we understand what we have observed in God's Word and realize that the lessons are true, then there must be ways in which we can put the truth of Scripture into practice in our personal lives.

- Work through the list of teachings one more time, answering the personal question that begins with *therefore* for each of the sections. In other words, ask the question, "I understand that Jesus meant for me to be salt and light in my world and make a difference, therefore I will _____."

5:13–16 Salt and Light

_____

_____

_____

_____

_____

_____

_____

_____

_____

_____

5:17–20 Jesus on the Law

_____

_____

_____

_____

_____

_____

_____

_____

_____

_____

5:21–26 Deadly Intent

_____

_____

_____

_____

_____

_____

_____

_____

_____

_____

5:27–30 Adultery

_____
_____
_____
_____
_____
_____
_____
_____
_____
_____
_____
_____

5:31–32 Divorce

_____
_____
_____
_____
_____
_____
_____
_____
_____
_____
_____
_____

5:33–37 Promises

_____
_____
_____
_____
_____
_____
_____
_____
_____
_____
_____
_____

• In what area of your life right now do you most feel the need to experience the compassion of Jesus?

_____

_____

_____

_____

_____

_____

_____

_____

_____

_____

Choices

Coming to conclusions remains an exercise in reflection until you decide on a plan of action and actually take a step of faith.

• Which two of the conclusions above require the most immediate and radical attention in your life?

_____

_____

_____

_____

_____

_____

_____

_____

_____

_____

_____

_____

• What person could you entrust with the responsibility of holding you accountable to follow through on these conclusions by 1) telling them what you are working on; 2) asking them to pray for you; and 3) giving them permission to check on your progress?

_____

_____

_____

_____

_____

_____

_____

_____

_____

_____

_____

_____

• In what other ways would you desire to see these lessons from Jesus become a reality in your own life?

_____

_____

_____

_____

_____

_____

_____

_____

_____

_____

_____

_____

_____

_____

_____

_____

_____

_____

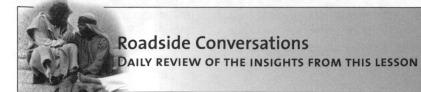

Roadside Conversations
DAILY REVIEW OF THE INSIGHTS FROM THIS LESSON

Daily Roadside Conversation 1
"Light Taste"

READ: Matthew 5:13–16
Reflect on this key question:
In what ways am I aware that I live my life in the spotlight of God's care and direction?

_____

_____

_____

_____

_____

_____

_____

_____

_____

_____

_____

_____

Resolve to ask God for increased spotlight-consciousness, an awareness that He is with you at every moment in your life.

Suggested prayer: Lord Jesus, one of the last promises You gave Your disciples was that You would be with us always. I want that to be more than just words in my life. I know they are true, but I want to live out their truth. I want to be aware of You as I would be aware of a spotlight shining on me, affecting the way I see everyone and everything else. I also give You permission to shine through me and flavor the world with my life, whatever the cost may be. In Your name, Jesus. Amen.

Daily Roadside Conversation 2
"Authority"

READ: Matthew 5:17–20
Reflect on this key question:
What evidence would others find in my life if they were closely examining me to see if I really seek to live by God's Word?

_____

_____

_____

_____

_____

_____

_____

_____

_____

_____

Resolve to identify areas in which God's Word has not been allowed to speak into your life and make some specific, intentional changes there (finances? sharing your faith? prayer life? participating in church life?).

Suggested prayer: Lord, I live in a world that rejects absolutes. My culture seems to live in direct contradiction to almost everything You said in this part of the Sermon on the Mount. I realize that if I begin to live openly and enthusiastically by Your values, I will certainly experience the last of the Beatitudes. Never allow me to avoid obedience to You out of fear of what the world may say or think. Teach me to honor Your Word by obeying it! As my Lord, You are my Authority, my Master. Amen.

Daily Roadside Conversation 3
"Murder Without a Body"
READ: Matthew 5:21–26
Reflect on this key question:
How does Jesus want me to respond to and resolve the tide of rage that can surge in my life when I've been misunderstood, mistreated, or hurt?

_____

_____

_____

_____

_____

_____

_____

_____

_____

_____

Resolve to identify anger quickly, and ask the Lord for help in expressing what needs to be expressed while controlling the manner, the magnitude, and the limits of anger.

Suggested prayer: Lord Jesus, I know You understand anger. You experienced it and expressed it wisely and justly. I also know that most of what angers me turns out to be trivial. Teach me, Lord, to be angry yet not to sin (Eph. 4:26). Help me question my anger rather than assume that it must be justified because it belongs to me. If anger is necessary, guide me in expressing it in a way that honors You. In Your name, Jesus. Amen.

what kind of man is this?

Daily Roadside Conversation 4
"Faithfulness"
READ: Matthew 5:27–30
Reflect on this key question:
How would I explain to someone that Jesus was more interested in obedience to the spirit of the Law than to the letter of the Law?

_____

_____

_____

_____

_____

_____

_____

_____

_____

_____

_____

_____

_____

_____

Resolve to refuse to settle for what looks good when it comes to obedience, and strive to live by what is good, even in what others can't see.

Suggested prayer: Jesus, I admit that it is easy to look down on the obvious failures of other people who struggle in areas that don't often affect me. But what would it be like if everyone could see my secret sins the way I see their public ones? My mind is a battlefield, and without Your constant help I lose battles every day. Forgive me for not trusting. You are my faithful ally. Thank You, Lord.

Daily Roadside Conversation 5
"Promises"
READ: Matthew 5:31–37
Reflect on this key question:
What relationships in my life have been seriously harmed by my failure to keep my word or follow through on my promises?

_____

_____

_____

_____

_____

_____

_____

_____

_____

_____

_____

_____

_____

Resolve to ask God for help in making things right wherever possible and guarding you against making promises you can't or won't keep.

Suggested prayer: Lord, help me to say and mean "yes" and "no." Train me to be the kind of person on whose word others can count. Help me to pay the price for failures so that I will remember the next time not to overstep my abilities, time, or strength. I want the quality of my words to reflect glory on Your promises, which are eternal. Thank You for keeping Your promises always, Lord.

ENEMIES AND OTHER STRANGERS

Key Question for This Lesson:
How did Jesus expect His followers to conduct themselves in the world?

introduction

"That was then; this is now."

Six times in the Sermon on the Mount Jesus used the expression, "You have heard that it was said." He followed up each of these statements with the phrase, "But I tell you." His point, of course, never was to change the Law but to help people see what the Law really meant. He showed people that their past understanding and applications of God's Word were often flawed or incomplete. He refused to let a mistaken tradition stand in the way of the truth.

Jesus lived in a culture that interpreted God's Law as a superficial list of legalistic standards, which were manipulated for the benefit of those in power. He tore up the list. He shattered the standards. He made God's Law once again an awesome and fearful thing. He pointed out the absolute character of God's Law. He destroyed people's ability to justify themselves by shallow efforts to "keep the law." He made repentance and grace a necessity. No wonder He drew such strong responses from people.

In the last session, we looked at the way Jesus applied the Law to our closest relationships—family, marriage, and friendships. In this les-

son, we turn to His teaching about our responsibilities in the world. These apply to enemies and other strangers. They also apply to our contact points in the world—prayer, fasting, and money. The Sermon on the Mount demonstrates its timelessness in the way these teaching points directly touch our lives. "That was then; this is now" doesn't necessarily mean that the past was wrong. It may mean that the present is wrong and needs to be brought into line with the past. In either case, Jesus makes clear that God's truth—right down to the smallest detail—remains absolute, unchangeable, in force. We are accountable to God's Word.

THE POWER
AND THE
PRESENCE
Visual Bible Study

The law Jesus refers to is the law of the old covenant, not a new law, but the same law which He quoted to the rich young man and the lawyer when they wanted to know the revealed will of God. It becomes a new law only because it is Christ who binds His followers to it. For Christians, therefore, the law is not a "better law" than that of the Pharisees, but one and the same; every letter of it, every jot and tittle, must remain in force and be observed until the end of the world. But there is a "better righteousness" which is expected of Christians. Without it none can enter into the kingdom of heaven, for it is the indispensable condition of discipleship. None can have this better righteousness but those to whom Christ is speaking here, those whom He has called. The call of Christ, in fact Christ Himself, is the *sine qua non* of this better righteousness.

Now we can see why up to now Jesus has said nothing about Himself in the Sermon on the Mount. Between the disciples and the better righteousness demanded of them stands the Person of Christ, who came to fulfill the law of the old covenant. This is the fundamental presupposition of the whole Sermon on the Mount. Jesus manifests His perfect union with the will of God as revealed in the Old Testament law and prophets. He has in fact nothing to add to the commandments of God, except this, that He keeps them. He fulfills the law, and He tells us so Himself, therefore it must be true. He fulfills the law down to the last iota.

~*Dietrich Bonhoeffer*[1]

To Get Started

Use one or more of the questions below to begin to focus your thinking on the themes of this session. Use the lines provided to jot down ideas, and be prepared to share with others in the group.

• How has *The Visual Bible* affected the way you read your Bible?

_____

• What has been your most memorable moment from seeing and hearing the Bible presented in this way?

_____

• How would you describe your earliest experience in which you learned the meaning of responsibility?

_____

_____

_____

_____

_____

_____

_____

_____

_____

_____

_____

_____

_____

_____

_____

_____

• What do you think are a Christian's three or four most important responsibilities in his or her relationship with God?

_____

_____

_____

_____

_____

_____

_____

_____

_____

_____

_____

_____

_____

_____

_____

_____

_____

_____

Watching the Word
The Visual Bible "Reading" 3

As you may have done in the last session, use the spaces in First Impressions to make notes during the video presentation. Again, note particularly the way in which the account shifts back and forth between Matthew, the Gospel narrator, and Jesus Himself. How do you think these alternating presentations help or hinder the clarity of the storytelling?

○ Video Segment: Matthew 6:1—7:29
○ Study Text: Matthew 5:38—6:24

First Impressions

The Visual Bible seeks to communicate the text of Scripture faithfully while at the same time capturing an accurate idea of what the surroundings and environment might have been like. The Scriptures come with few "stage notes." This section allows you to reflect on the video presentation itself.

• One of the unusual features of *The Visual Bible* is the exploration of humorous possibilities in the accounts. As you notice unique features of this presentation, jot down any humorous components that affect the story. Do you find these realistic or out of place?

5:38–42 Revenge

_____

_____

_____

_____

_____

_____

_____

5:43–48 Loving Enemies

_____

_____

_____

_____

_____

_____

_____

6:1–4 Helping Others

_____

_____

_____

_____

_____

_____

_____

6:5–15 How to Pray

_____
_____
_____
_____
_____
_____
_____
_____
_____

6:16–18 Fasting

_____
_____
_____
_____
_____
_____
_____
_____
_____
_____

6:19–24 Treasures

_____
_____
_____
_____
_____
_____
_____
_____
_____

Second Look

- Write out a brief summary of the main points in each of the sections:
  5:38–42 Revenge

_____
_____
_____
_____
_____
_____
_____
_____
_____
_____

5:43–48 Loving Enemies

6:1–4 Helping Others

6:5–15 How to Pray

6:16–18 Fasting

6:19–24 Treasures

Observations

The key theme of this lesson has to do with responsibility. As you move through the study steps that lead to personal application, note the way in which Jesus touched on various aspects of life and indicated that He expected His disciples to be fully engaged, responsible participants in the world. He expected them to respond according to His example and directions.

- In what ways do the following passages indicate that Jesus placed specific and important responsibilities into the hands of His followers?

5:38–42 Revenge

_____
_____
_____
_____
_____
_____
_____
_____

5:43–48 Loving Enemies

_____
_____
_____
_____
_____
_____
_____
_____

6:1–4 Helping Others

_____
_____
_____
_____
_____
_____
_____

6:5–15 How to Pray

_____
_____
_____
_____
_____
_____
_____

6:16–18 Fasting

_____

_____

_____

_____

_____

_____

_____

_____

6:19–24 Treasures

_____

_____

_____

_____

_____

_____

_____

_____

Conclusions

The video clip for this session has already reminded us that Jesus knew His audience would respond in one of two different ways: 1) either put His words into action, or 2) do nothing with His teaching. The results in their lives, Jesus said, could be accurately predicted. Since we have no reason to believe that any of Jesus' instructions have been annulled by time, the responsibility to clearly understand and act on His expectations faces us every day. Review each of the sections from this study as you thoughtfully work through the following questions.

• For each of the passages in this session, write out a personal application conclusion based on Jesus' teaching.

5:38–42 Revenge—My responsibilities are to . . .

_____

_____

_____

_____

_____

_____

_____

5:43–48 Loving Enemies—My responsibilities are to . . .

_____

_____

_____

_____

_____

_____

_____

6:1–4 Helping Others—My responsibilities are to . . .

_____
_____
_____
_____
_____
_____
_____
_____
_____

6:5–15 How to Pray—My responsibilities are to . . .

_____
_____
_____
_____
_____
_____
_____
_____
_____
_____
_____

6:16–18 Fasting—My responsibilities are to . . .

_____
_____
_____
_____
_____
_____
_____
_____
_____
_____

6:19–24 Treasures—My responsibilities are to . . .

_____
_____
_____
_____
_____
_____
_____
_____
_____

Choices

The final step in the application process involves the question, "So what?" After you have examined, thought about, studied, and discussed Jesus' teaching, there still remains a decision you alone can make. Will you live by His words or walk away and continue to live as you always have? What you do will probably depend on how prepared you feel to face the storms of life. Will your "house" stand the wind and the rain?

- Choose one of the above conclusions as a starting point in putting Jesus' commands into action. Which one did you choose, and what do you plan to do?

_____

_____

_____

_____

_____

_____

_____

_____

_____

_____

_____

_____

_____

_____

_____

_____

_____

_____

_____

_____

_____

_____

_____

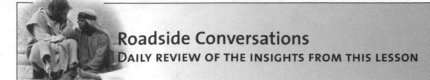

Roadside Conversations
DAILY REVIEW OF THE INSIGHTS FROM THIS LESSON

Daily Roadside Conversation 1
"Open Hands"

> **READ:** Matthew 5:38–42
>
> Reflect on this key question:
>
> *In my life experiences, when have I seen the wisdom of Jesus' directions against personal retaliation proven true?*

_____

_____

_____

_____

_____

_____

_____

_____

_____

_____

_____

Resolve to evaluate your present friendships and relationships, looking for places in which you have not responded in a Christlike way, in order to make corrections.

Suggested prayer: Jesus, in Your own trial and death You certainly showed us a life that didn't seek retaliation. I realize that in my own strength, that kind of forgiveness is not in me. I don't want to turn the other cheek or walk a second mile. I know that if I do these things it will be because You have made it possible. Lord, help me to respond as You responded; help me to be like You. In Your name I pray. Amen.

Daily Roadside Conversation 2
"Lovable Opponent"

> **READ:** Matthew 5:43–48
>
> Reflect on this key question:
>
> *As I seek to take Jesus' commands seriously, how does the way I feel toward my enemies affect what the Lord has told me to do?*

_____

_____

_____

_____

_____

_____

_____

_____

_____

_____

Resolve to identify those people in your life that you feel least inclined to pray for, and create a prayer list with those names.

Suggested prayer: Lord, I need to learn what it means to love. My definition has so much to do with feeling a certain way that it's hard for me to think that You might want me to treat an enemy with love despite my feelings. I know You chose the nails and the cross, not because You felt good about those things, but because You saw something great beyond them. Help me to see life that way. Amen.

Daily Roadside Conversation 3
"Undercover Generosity"

READ: Matthew 6:1–4
Reflect on this key question:
How many examples can I think of when I have practiced a random act of kindness without being noticed by anyone? What was the outcome?

_____

_____

_____

_____

_____

_____

_____

_____

_____

_____

_____

Resolve to go out of your way in the next week to take private action that will help others who will never know where the help originated.

Suggested prayer: Lord Jesus, lead me to someone unexpectedly today, and at some point during our encounter, impress upon me something that I can do for that person in Your name. Help me resist the temptation to let that person know what I'm going to do. Help me carry out some undercover generosity today. In Your name, Jesus. Amen.

Daily Roadside Conversation 4
"When You Pray"

READ: Matthew 6:5–15
Reflect on this key question:
To what degree have I thought through each of the phrases in the Lord's Prayer, so that I have specific ideas in mind when I pray?

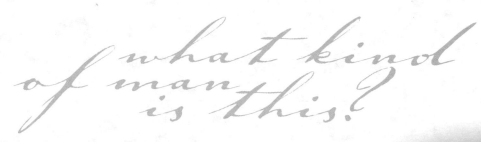

what kind of man is this?

_____
_____
_____
_____
_____
_____
_____
_____
_____
_____
_____
_____
_____
_____
_____
_____
_____

Resolve to use the Lord's Prayer more often as an outline to keep your prayers from becoming rote or self-centered.

Suggested prayer: Jesus, thank You for teaching us how to pray. Thank You for also showing us how an intimate relationship with our Heavenly Father changes all of life. Thank You for giving us a pattern for prayer. Help me remember to put it into practice. Thank You, Lord.

Daily Roadside Conversation 5
"Financial Diet"

READ: Matthew 6:16–24
Reflect on this key question:
What evidence is there in my life that I am a steward of, rather than a slave to, my treasures?

_____
_____
_____
_____
_____
_____
_____
_____
_____
_____
_____
_____
_____
_____
_____
_____

Resolve to take specific steps regularly (like tithing), not in a legalistic way, but in a practical way to remind yourself that earthly treasures, no matter how great their value, are not eternal.

Suggested prayer: Lord, I don't want to have a divided allegiance. I don't want to pretend to serve You while I'm really serving my own purposes. I want to be Your servant. Point out to me when my behavior is inconsistent with what I want to be. Help me always to keep my heart and my treasures first and foremost in Your hands. I ask you this in Your name, Jesus. Amen.

THE HIDDEN LIFE

Key Question for This Lesson:
What is the relationship between faith and obedience?

introduction

"But, what shall we eat?"

"What shall we drink?"

"What shall we wear?"

For most of us, these questions are actually hyperbole. They're exaggerations. We don't mean them literally. What we actually mean is, "Will we get to eat what we like? Will we get our favorite drinks? Will we get to wear stylish clothes?" Most of us don't have to worry about basic needs; we worry about preferences.

Someone sarcastically pointed out that the worst kind of worry is middle-class worry. The poor worry about what they don't have. The rich worry about what they do have. But the middle class worry about both what they have and don't have. When we worry for any reason, Jesus pointed out, we are acting like pagans, like people who don't believe.

In the final six sections of the Sermon on the Mount, Jesus spent most of His time giving directions about what we might call our "hidden life." These are not necessarily new themes, but they are emphasized in a new way. The Beatitudes certainly have their root and greatest effect in our inner person. Many of the insights about relationships and responsibilities that we looked at in the last two sessions have to do with maintaining a consistency between our internal life and our external living. These final words from Jesus highlight and apply His command that we be, first and foremost, seekers of God's kingdom and God's righteousness in every part of our lives.

Don't miss David Jeremiah's closing challenge after the video clip from *The Visual Bible*. He notes, "As you think about and discuss these final thoughts from the Sermon on the Mount, put yourself in the place of someone in the crowd. What did they take away with them that day? Did they realize who had been speaking to them? Did they decide which kind of house they were going to build with their lives? What did you hear Jesus saying to you?"

THE POWER
AND THE
PRESENCE

Visual Bible Study

In this connection one injunction is thrice repeated. "Be not anxious" (vv. 25, 31, 34). This is the all-inclusive word. It is illustrated, emphasized, argued, with inimitable skill by the great Master and Teacher Himself. It accurately defines the whole attitude of mind which His disciples should maintain toward necessary things. "Take not thought" was a most unhappy mistranslation, for, as we shall see before we have finished, that is exactly what the King did not mean. All His argument as to our attitude being characterized by freedom from anxiety, is based upon the fact of our ability to take thought. He does not hint for a single moment that we are to be careless or improvident. That against which He charged His disciples, and still charges us, is carking [burdensome] care, the care which means fretting, worry, restlessness, feverishness; or perhaps, better than all, in the simple terms of the Revision, "Anxiety." "Be not anxious." There are things of this life which are necessary, which, so far as we know, have no place in the larger life toward which we go. Food, drink, raiment, are necessary things, but are not provided for us by God apart from our own thought, our own endeavor, our own activity. But none of these things is to produce anxiety in the hearts of the subjects of the King.

~G. Campbell Morgan[1]

To Get Started

Use the questions below to begin to focus your thinking on the themes of this session. Use the lines provided to jot down ideas, and be prepared to share with others in the group.

• In retrospect, what is the silliest thing you ever worried about?

_____

_____

_____

_____

_____

_____

_____

_____

_____

_____

• What are your most significant recurring worries?

_____

_____

_____

_____

_____

_____

_____

_____

_____

_____

_____

• Once you have realized you are worrying about something, what do you usually do next? How do you deal with worry?

_____

_____

_____

_____

_____

_____

_____

_____

_____

_____

_____

_____

_____

_____

_____

_____

_____

_____

• If you had to describe your typical day by assigning every thought or action to one of two categories—external life or internal life—what percentage would each of those categories receive?

_____

_____

_____

_____

_____

_____

_____

_____

_____

_____

_____

_____

_____

_____

_____

_____

_____

Watching the Word
The Visual Bible "Reading" 4

Though you may have already noticed this feature, pay careful attention during this session's clip from *The Visual Bible* to the pace of Jesus' presentation. Experiment once in a while with reading Scripture like this yourself. How does the pace help or hinder your understanding of what Jesus is saying?

○ Video Segment: Matthew 6:1—7:29
○ Study Text: Matthew 6:25—7:29

First Impressions

Jesus probably said, and you have probably heard, the teachings in the Sermon on the Mount many times. Try to imagine what it would be like to hear them for the first time. Perhaps some parts of your exposure to *The Visual Bible* have actually felt like a first impression. You may not think you have ever heard Jesus' words in quite this way before. Those first impressions may lead to some amazing discoveries and changes in your life.

• For each of the sections in this study, note any comments, questions, or observations that you would like to bring up later for discussion.

6:25–34 No Worries

_____

_____

_____

_____

_____

_____

_____

_____

_____

_____

_____

7:1–6 Deconstructive Criticism

_____

_____

_____

_____

_____

_____

_____

_____

_____

_____

_____

_____

7:7–12 Persistence

_____
_____
_____
_____
_____
_____
_____
_____
_____
_____
_____
_____

7:13–14 The Way

_____
_____
_____
_____
_____
_____
_____
_____
_____
_____
_____
_____
_____
_____

7:15–20 Fruitfulness

_____
_____
_____
_____
_____
_____
_____
_____
_____
_____
_____
_____
_____
_____
_____
_____

7:21–29 House Builders

_____
_____
_____
_____
_____
_____
_____
_____
_____
_____
_____

Second Look

Before we can talk about the meaning of Scripture, we have to make sure we actually see what is there. These questions are designed to help you summarize briefly the teaching from each of these sections of Scripture.

• What is the central point, command, or lesson in each of these passages?

6:25–34 No Worries

_____
_____
_____
_____
_____
_____
_____
_____
_____
_____
_____

7:1–6 Deconstructive Criticism

_____
_____
_____
_____
_____
_____
_____
_____
_____
_____

7:7–12 Persistence

7:13–14 The Way

7:15–20 Fruitfulness

> So Jesus confronts us with himself, sets before us the radical choice between obedience and disobedience, and calls us to an unconditional commitment of mind, will, and life to his teaching. The way he does it is to warn us of two unacceptable alternatives, first a merely verbal profession (21–23) and secondly a merely intellectual knowledge (24–27). Neither can be a substitute for obedience; indeed each may be a camouflage for disobedience. Jesus emphasizes with great solemnity that on a thoroughgoing obedience our eternal destiny depends.
> ~John R. W. Stott[2]

7:21–29 House Builders

_____
_____
_____
_____
_____
_____
_____
_____
_____
_____
_____
_____
_____

Observations

What a startling experience that must have been, to listen to someone and realize, each time your eyes met, that He knew you better than you knew yourself. Bruce Marchiano did an excellent job in conveying hints of that quality of perception that was part of Jesus' interaction with people. He answered their questions and disarmed their arguments and excuses before they were made. He brought His sermon to a stunning conclusion with the announcement that delight or disaster awaited every person who had heard His words, depending on what they did with them.

• Keeping in mind the title of this lesson, _The Hidden Life,_ how do each of these passages convey the importance of obedience in a part of our internal relationship with God?

6:25–34 No Worries

_____
_____
_____
_____
_____
_____
_____
_____
_____
_____
_____

7:1–6 Deconstructive Criticism

_____
_____
_____
_____
_____
_____
_____
_____
_____
_____
_____
_____

7:7–12 Persistence

_____
_____
_____
_____
_____
_____
_____
_____
_____
_____
_____
_____
_____
_____

7:13–14 The Way

_____
_____
_____
_____
_____
_____
_____
_____
_____
_____
_____
_____

7:15–20 Fruitfulness

_____
_____
_____
_____
_____
_____
_____
_____
_____
_____

7:21–29 House Builders

_____
_____
_____
_____
_____
_____
_____
_____
_____
_____
_____
_____

Conclusions

Having witnessed the Sermon on the Mount in _The Visual Bible,_ we can safely conclude that Jesus was a captivating and entertaining speaker. But He never settled for being merely entertaining. He was too pointed, too truthful, and too aware of His audience's real needs to let them simply go away entertained. He sent them away with directions and challenges. He told them that hearing wasn't nearly enough. He insisted that they act. He promised a life that would stand up to the storms if they would trust Him and carry out His instructions. Work on the following questions as part of your hidden life construction.

• Before you can address the lives of others, what habits need to be corrected in you to bring your hidden life into line with Christ's teaching?

_____
_____
_____
_____
_____
_____
_____
_____
_____
_____

• Identify one persistent worry that you intend to turn over to God as an expression of trust.

_____

_____

_____

_____

_____

_____

_____

_____

_____

• What part(s) of your hidden life in Christ do you think need(s) some specific attention this week?

_____

_____

_____

_____

_____

_____

_____

_____

_____

_____

_____

Choices

Good intentions are rarely enough to bring us to action. Even a simple plan that involves two or three specific steps has a much better chance to move us from intention to action. We rarely plan to fail; we simply fail to plan. Choices involve the planning stage. How will you put your conclusions into action?

• Below are three spaces for action plans relating to each of the Conclusion questions above. Try to note at least two specific steps you can take to put each of your conclusions into action this week.

Changing how I think about the lives of others:

_____

_____

_____

_____

_____

_____

_____

_____

_____

Turning a major worry over to God:

_____

_____

_____

_____

_____

_____

_____

_____

_____

Specific attention to a part of my hidden life this week:

_____

_____

_____

_____

_____

_____

_____

_____

_____

_____

_____

_____

- How has this presentation of Jesus' Sermon on the Mount helped you appreciate the Lord in new ways? How has your relationship with Jesus been affected? What insight from these lessons have you already put into action in your life?

_____

_____

_____

_____

_____

_____

_____

_____

_____

_____

_____

_____

Roadside Conversations
DAILY REVIEW OF THE INSIGHTS FROM THIS LESSON

Daily Roadside Conversation 1
"Lilies Don't Worry"

READ: Matthew 6:25–34

Reflect on this key question:

In the long run, will I be better off running after what pagans run after or running after Christ?

_____

_____

_____

_____

_____

_____

_____

_____

_____

_____

_____

_____

Resolve to ask a trusted friend to help identify areas in life in which your concerns are not in line with what Jesus calls important.

Suggested prayer: Lord, I honestly admit I don't have a complete idea of what it means to seek first Your kingdom and Your righteousness. I guess *kingdom* implies that You're in charge, and *righteousness* means that Your orders are to be obeyed. I really don't want to worry about things that don't matter. Keep me running after You, every day of my life. In Your name I pray. Amen.

Daily Roadside Conversation 2
"Two-Way Measuring Cup"

READ: Matthew 7:1–6

Reflect on this key question:

Thinking about the last two or three people I criticized, how would I measure up if I used the same standard on myself?

_____

_____

_____

_____

_____

_____

_____

_____

_____

_____

_____

Resolve to give people the benefit of the doubt, question your own motives, and resist quick or careless evaluations of others.

Suggested prayer: Lord Jesus, I realize in a new way how much of life involves measuring other people. It's unavoidable. Help me to be a truthful measurer of others, always remembering that the standard I use on others will be used on me. And thank You for loving and saving me even though I could never measure up to Your holy standard. Amen.

Daily Roadside Conversation 3
"Ask . . . Seek . . . Knock"
READ: Matthew 7:7–12
Reflect on this key question:
How many examples can I think of that involve my moving beyond asking to seeking and knocking in my relationship with God?

_____

_____

_____

_____

_____

_____

_____

_____

_____

_____

_____

_____

Resolve to set aside more time for prayer, Bible study, and application of what God shows you in His Word.

Suggested prayer: Lord Jesus, help me to ask persistently in accordance with Your will. Help me to seek Your will persistently in Your Word. Help me to knock persistently by acting on Your will. I anticipate the great and good things You will provide for me. In Your name, Jesus. Amen.

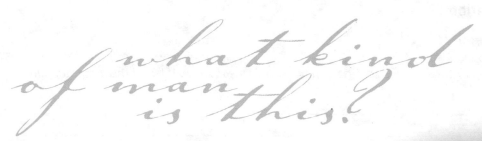

what kind of man is this?

Daily Roadside Conversation 4
"Tight Squeeze"
READ: Matthew 7:13–14
Reflect on this key question:
How many things from this life (like worries) have I tried to carry with me through the narrow gate and on the narrow road only to discover they won't fit?

_____

_____

_____

_____

_____

_____

_____

_____

_____

_____

_____

_____

_____

Resolve to find ways to "let go" of the things that have too great a hold on you in this life, those things that take away from your ability to value what Christ calls important.

Suggested prayer: Jesus, I could never have found the narrow gate, nor can I walk the narrow way, without Your help. Point out to me those things in my life that don't fit in Your plans. Give me the strength to drop them by the wayside. Thank you, Lord.

Daily Roadside Conversation 5
"Storm-Proof Construction"
READ: Matthew 7:21–29
Reflect on this key question:
How did the structure of my life hold up in the last storm? In what ways can I anchor more firmly to Christ, the solid Rock?

_____

_____

_____

_____

_____

_____

_____

_____

_____

_____

_____

_____

Resolve to return often to the Sermon on the Mount until you are familiar with this concentrated dose of Jesus' teaching.

Suggested prayer: Lord, thank You for Your teaching in the Sermon. I feel just like Your first audience, who were amazed by Your teaching. You are my Authority. Now help me carry out the plans and choices I've made throughout this study so that Your authority becomes a reality in my life. I ask You this in Your name, Jesus. Amen.

NOTES

LESSON 1
THE BIG PICTURE

1. Clarence Jordan, *Sermon on the Mount* (Valley Forge: Judson Press, 1952), 15.
2. Earl D. Radmacher, Th.D., ed., *The Nelson Study Bible* (Nashville: Thomas Nelson, Inc., 1997).
3. Bruce B. Barton et al., *Life Application Bible Commentary: Matthew* (Wheaton: Tyndale House Publishers, Inc., 1996), 76.

LESSON 2
LIFE IN THE SPOTLIGHT

1. Myron S. Augsburger, *Matthew* in *Mastering the New Testament,* ed. L. J. Ogilvie (Dallas: Word Inc., 1982), 67–68.
2. Eugene H. Peterson, *The Message: The New Testament in Contemporary English* (Colorado Springs: NavPress Publishing Group, 1993), 18.

LESSON 3
ENEMIES AND OTHER STRANGERS

1. Dietrich Bonhoeffer, *The Cost of Discipleship* (New York: The Macmillan Company, 1959), 110–11.
2. John R. W. Stott, *Christian Counter-Culture: The Message of the Sermon on the Mount* (Downers Grove: InterVarsity Press, 1978), 115.

LESSON 4
THE HIDDEN LIFE

1. G. Campbell Morgan, *The Gospel According to Matthew* (New York: Fleming H. Revell Company, 1929), 67.
2. John R. W. Stott, *Christian Counter-Culture: The Message of the Sermon on the Mount* (Downers Grove: InterVarsity Press, 1978), 205.